Over the Village

poems by

Susan Gunter

Finishing Line Press
Georgetown, Kentucky

Over the Village

Copyright © 2022 by Susan Gunter
ISBN 978-1-64662-937-4 First Edition
All rights reserved under International and Pan-American Copyright Conventions. No part of this book may be reproduced in any manner whatsoever without written permission from the publisher, except in the case of brief quotations embodied in critical articles and reviews.

ACKNOWLEDGMENTS

"Sestina for Esther" in *Poet Lore*, 1988
"Composition: Mixed Media" in *Burning House Press*, England, 2018
"Requiem for a Piano Teacher" in *Louisville Review*, 2017
"Stitching a Mourning Garment in *Emrys*, 2020
"Spring Song" in *From the Green Horseshoe: Poems by James Dickey's Students*, 1985
"Ponce de Leon" in *College English*, 1996
"August 10, 1995" in *BYU Quarterly*, 1995
"Donna" in *Semaphore*, 2015
"Digging Rutabagas" in *Rocky Mountain Review*, 1993
"Apple Time" in *Marin Poetry Center Anthology*, 2020

Publisher: Leah Huete de Maines
Editor: Christen Kincaid
Cover Art: Susan Gunter
Author Photo: William Gunter
Cover Design: Elizabeth Maines McCleavy

Order online: www.finishinglinepress.com
also available on amazon.com

Author inquiries and mail orders:
Finishing Line Press
PO Box 1626
Georgetown, Kentucky 40324
USA

Table of Contents

Over the Village 1

Sestina for Esther 2

Word Perfect 4

Painting my Grandmother's House 5

Composition: Mixed Media 6

Requiem for a Piano Teacher 7

Stitching a Mourning Garment 8

Spring Song 9

Exterminator 10

Ponce de Leon 11

August 10, 1995 12

Donna 15

Digging Rutabagas 17

Apple Time 19

For My Beloved William

Over the Village

I am one of those women
in a Chagall mural
flying over bright rooftops—
except my palette is darker.
I look down at my mother's
twisted skinny leg,
her incestuous cousin love,
a mad uncle gone
blackberrying,
suicides here—
alcoholics there—
detritus piling up
in a rat's nest of
Swedish relatives.

I sail over them,
conjuring up
the magical parts
of my childhoods
that happen even
in families that
eat their children:
the doll's house made
of cardboard and
wallpaper scraps,
the watercress stream
bubbling in the woods,
pitting cherries
with a curved hairpin,
finding seven-leaf clovers,
sawing on my fiddle
as doves fly up
from the moon,
flying flying away.

Sestina for Esther

The first thing that I remember is a house.
Curved sunbursts circled the long porch
and lilacs shaded the sweet gnarled garden.
At night the house set free its ghosts,
so I hid beneath the covers, keeping still.
They breathed so hard I thought they were in pain.

The old ones in the rooms knew about pain.
They said, in the end, it came to every house.
They said I'd learn someday, but still
I wouldn't believe them. I read on the porch,
fairy stories whose endings were free of ghosts
and whose journeys took me to a far enchanted garden.

At twilight, catching fireflies in the garden,
I'd put them in a jar. Was there pain
for them, or were they invincible as ghosts?
After the stars came out, I went into the house,
leaving the mayonnaise jar on the porch.
In the morning all the fireflies were still.

Mason jars lined the cellar shelves, distilled
brandy, cherries, spiced peaches from the garden.
Against the stonewall the striped canvas porch
swing rested from summer storms. Discarded pain
remedies were thrown beneath the stairs. The house
swayed above those restless moaning ghosts.

I wish I'd stop dreaming about those ghosts.
I wish that my mother were still
in the kitchen, baking bread in the house
and canning the wealth of her late summer's garden.
I wish she had withstood the pain
that made her jump from a beam on the porch.

All their warnings came true on the porch.
Then I knew what the old ones meant. The ghosts
had condemned her to a twilight world of pain.
After she jumped, all their voices were still.
Weeds choked her yellow roses in the garden
and the white paint peeled from the house.

Word Perfect

In this black and white snapshot
it's not yet spring—the branches
on the shrubs flanking the house
are at the dark end of the value scale,
the white of the clown's shoe
next to me at the light end.
The concrete steps rise behind me,
shadowed obstacles guarding
the house. I am in overalls,
short sleeves, and there's no
snow on the ground. I think
it is 1950; I have just turned
three. My mouth opens wide.
I appear to be screaming,
possibly in delight, as I balance
a large book on my lap.
My hair lifts in curls above
my moon-shaped face,
my eyes staring hard at the
catalpa tree, which is just
beyond the frame. I already
know who I will be: reader,
writer, loud chronicler of
the ones absent from the photo,
the others whose histories will take
a lifetime for me to record.

Painting My Grandmother's House

I lay down washes, darkening
and deepening them at the top
of the sky, thinning at the horizon,
intensifying again as they slip
to the bottom of my canvas.

Where the mountains vee, I see a house.
The snow above looks as though
it might slide into it,
carrying it far down the hill
in a jumble of timber and stone.
Pillows of snow cover the rocks
around it, freezing in crevices
and expanding when the sun comes back.
Freeze, thaw. Freeze, thaw, nature's
alteration so slow we scarcely see it.

Time alters us, too, rolling us down
the hill to a cliff towering over
the bottom of eternity, then
winding up our years like balls
of yarn, until only the house
in the painting and the shapes
haunting its windows remain.

Composition: Mixed Media

I paint to learn what my eyes barely see,
things hidden to me: cast shadows, a latch,
my mother's ghost floating behind the drapes.

I study the image I shot, its hues and patterns:
copper door, stained windows, the stone of walls

and sun faded stone, the blur of a doorway's curve.

I sketch the door. I mask it. I pour
Holbein's opera rose over phthalo blue.
My scumbling reveals the shapes.

I'm not done. My three hundred pound

cold press needs to dry. I eye it in the mirror
to see whether I like it better backwards.

Like Dodgson's Alice, I've found a world.
Once I was young; I lost someone. I glaze
a viridian on top of my pain: I paint a door.

Requiem for a Piano Teacher

It was the first death for her—and for me—
my first funeral, first time in a pagan church,
the communion wine trickling down chins
like blood red tears, melismata of grief,
flickering waxen prayers, gilded idolatry
                                  nothing like Methodist ritual.

I walked to her clapboard house each week,
its black and white shutters like her keyboard
where black keys threw tiny shadows
onto white octaves. Her sacramental fingers
tapped a new alphabet, teaching me to read
                                  that women could live alone.

Death found Miss Cartney one hot August,
the parlor piano silent, the sheet music closed,
                                  the metronome stopped.

Now her memory shades into my mother's,
both their lives relics, printed scores too difficult
for me to learn by heart. But I still smell
the gold and silver stars she pasted in my book,
                                  that wet odor of mucilage.

I can scarcely write far enough away from them—
they hover too near. I let the wafer of regret dissolve
                              on my tongue.

Stitching a Mourning Garment
—*for Carl Evar Ropp, 1931-1932*

She chose from the fabrics in her bureau,
bolts of chenille furred like caterpillars,
gold-figured brocades, woolen baizes,
watered silks as soft as birds' wings.

She measured the yards hand to nose
pinked the bombazine's edges—no time
to finish her seams—matched notches
on the breast, wound her bobbin in black.

Thread snaking through the take up arm,
her foot pumped the treadle harder, faster
needle flashing in and out of the cloth
her thoughts unraveling in her head.

In the crib by her bed—still, silent
no gasping cry or shallow breath
no small form shivering, convulsing—
only a lily, his raiment bathed in light.

Spring Song

A fierce mantid monster grasps a naked twig,
divining in her garden the faint specter of spring.
She broods, then flings five hundred orphan eggs
all massed at the wind cold wall.
Her brawny pincer forelegs ape piety
as she waits, leaflike, for her helpless prey.
Her jaws grind slow rapacious circles.

This slender warrior waits to eat her mate.
She camouflages her hate with flower hues,
the colors of loyalty and deep love.
The male stumbles, blind and cold,
into her webbed deep nest.
The warrior moves to break his fall,
to break him, and black eyes watch
from out one thousand glassy panes.

They watch the praying mantis,
the eggs all dying in the wind,
her maw, her long prothorax,
her tensile life, his thorns.

Exterminator

I sit for long hot minutes watching the bees
in the amur maple trapped by greed, their
bodies hanging heavy in death's inertia.
It was my idea, having them hang there
swaying gently in the afternoon breeze,
their bodies massed darkly around the gaudy
green cone. I can't decide whether it
pleases me or not, though each dead body
means one less chance of being stung again.

I don't think I could kill a human, but
I've felt like it at times. My dad,
for example—I could have killed him
in the mental hospital in Kittanning, when
my mother said she'd rather live there
forever than go home. He just folded his arms
and set his jaw and wouldn't speak.
But after, after her funeral, after she burned
in the fire, he said he felt no guilt.
I wanted to smash him, stuff
him in the plastic bee cone,
but I didn't answer him.

Ponce de Leon

She knocks at our door,
her faded blue eyes,
like sky reflected in water,
wandering from side to side.

"Who is she?" I ask.
"What does she want?"
"It's that old woman again,"
my mother answers, whispering,

as if the calicoed
visitor could hear her.
I pull the curtain aside.
In her hand she holds bunches

of watercress in plastic bags.
I have seen that herb,
with its thin white flowers,
growing beneath the spring.

It smells of wet earth,
and it sprouts seeds shaped
like plump little hearts.
Floating on the stream,

it forms thick green clouds.
She knocks again. I see
that she carries tatted
handkerchiefs, maize and pink.

My mother turns from the window,
banishing her, that witch. But
we are all three alike—
female, suspect, mortal.

August 10, 1995

No one kept me from picking blackberries
that clear, sunlit August morning.
No one stopped me or called my name
when I stepped from the small cement porch,
ringed with morning glories and portulaca,
the small white dog running ahead of me
toward old man Guyowski's field.

Guyowski was dead now, but I knew him long ago,
when he was the janitor at the Polish Club
and his daughter Stella married my uncle Paul.
Every Friday night he stood at the entry
to the club, drunk and singing—
sometimes in broken English, sometimes in Polish.
I can see his small, crooked body still.
But that was in 1959, when I was someone else,
with no thought that I would ever leave
this small town with its muddy brown river,
oil-slicked, flowing through its center.

I followed the dog up the sloping hill,
past old Guyowski's pig stye,
a pile of odorless rocks and bricks
and ancient straw moldering in the cool air,
past his faded red barn, its double doors
crossed with gray splintered wood,
past the old fallow apple trees,
bent and heavy, their small windfall apples
with soft brown rotten spots dotting
their green translucent skin.
Was my skin green too that morning,
green with the sickly pallor
of days spent in the hospital, green
from the nights without sleep?

But I was alive, and I reached the field
below the barn, the dog still ahead of me.
Two rabbits, small and brown,
sprang from the bushes fringing the field,
and the dog started after them.
This was the place I'd longed all my life
to reach, the time and the place
where everything coalesced, as if I'd
been destined from birth to come here,
picking blackberries in the warm sun,
while my father breathed slow
and shallow breaths into a respirator,
making the float inside a plastic jar
rise a few scant inches at a time.

Yellowjackets swarmed in and out
of the shade, while I wandered along the field's
periphery, snatching the ripe blackberries
and piling them in my open palm,
sometimes mistaking the yet-unripened
red berries for raspberries,
until I tasted one and found it bitter.
All that I'd lost there—there in that town,
in that other life—all that I'd lost
suddenly rushed back, and I knew
that even those losses hadn't erased this place,
hadn't erased me from the place.
I was there in that field picking blackberries,
I was there in that cemetery,
some of my names engraved
on barely legible white stones,
and I was there in that hospital,
breathing up and down with my father.

At a time in my life when I feared
everyone I loved would leave me,
I came back to myself. I carried
my handful of berries back to the house
before the mother bear and her two cubs
caught me pilfering, or before
old man Guyowski's ghost floated
from the pig stye to tell me it was time,
while the sun still shone, to forgive my father.

Donna

When I think about her
(which isn't often any more)
I hear her jangling laugh
and see that brassy hair
twisted at the nape of her neck.
It's not as though
I didn't care for her—after all,
she was my uncle's wife.
But she was different
from us Swedes. Her maiden
name was Guyowski—
I couldn't even say it—
we saw her father drunk
every Friday night, standing
in front of the Polish Club.

Every weekday afternoon
Donna pulled on white gloves
and drove the Ford to town,
where she wandered through
the five and ten's musty aisles,
her spiked heels tapping
on those worn wooden floors.
Her lips shone bright red,
like a circus clown's
or even Marilyn Monroe's.
I overheard my mother
whisper at the ice cream social
that Donna's skirts were too tight.
Others must have thought so,
because all the men watched her
when she walked down Main Street.

One night, when I was asleep
in my cousin Janie's bedroom,
I woke to hear the screen door slam.
It was my uncle.
I heard him shouting at Donna,
but I couldn't hear her answer.
What could she have said?
After all, she was Polish
and he grew up on Swede Hill.
I heard the sound of glass breaking,
and finally, someone cried.
Was it my cousin, or me?

When she told us years later
she wished she had been a nun,
I didn't believe her.
But now, when I think
of how it all ended,
my uncle dying of cirrhosis
at fifty and Donna dry-eyed
beside his bed, still
wearing that painted smile,
I think the silence of convents
might have healed her.

Digging Rutabagas

in autumn,
earthy, tart,
a cold crop—
they tasted good with
horseradish spread,
my uncle told me.
I feared I wouldn't
like them, but I
didn't tell him that.
Instead I asked him
why he put forked sticks
between the apple branches.

Paperhanger by day,
he knew the town's houses
intimately, from their colors
and patterns. He moved among
their owners' narrow lives
with a lover's tenderness.

He gave me his scraps:
flocks, stripes, chintzes
for a dollhouse I'd made
from a cardboard box.
Sometimes I pretended
the box was my house,
and in that house of scraps
my mother and father
laughed and touched.

When I was thirteen
I wanted to know things
I couldn't find in books
(not even my biology text)
so I watched him often—
he wasn't married like
all the other grownups.

When I peered out my stair
window late at night
I saw his lamp burning.
Up reading Playboy,
the neighbors gossiped—
or is that what I remember
they said? It's been so long.

Years afterward, while
trying to write a sonnet
for someone I lost,
I made myself a rutabaga
sandwich. It left a bitter taste
that wouldn't go away.

Apple Time

A dividing line sunders before from after,
a before-the-apple-time from a time
that no one wants to come. But come it must.
And after the apple time, the resignation,
picking up the broken earthen shards,
the pottery strewn in fragments
along the burning orchard floor,
piecing them in the only possible fashion,
praying that the pot will hold
against the days to come, and come again,
each morning a cantus firmus
singing anger to despair.

Ever after I cannot remember
one single before-the-apple day,
one single green day
when I loved beyond tree fruit
my shining garden Eden.

Susan E. Gunter is a Professor of English Emerita and a three-time Fulbright Scholar. Her poems have appeared in journals in America, Bulgaria, England, Montenegro, and Sweden; her reviews have been published in *American Arts Quarterly, Crab Creek Review, the Harvard Review, Victorian Studies*, and other journals. In 2020 she won second place in the California State Poetry Society contest. She has also published three critically acclaimed academic books on the James family, including a biography of William. James's wife Alice, *Alice in Jamesland*. She held a fellowship in American Literature at Harvard's Houghton Library, 2004-2005, and fellowship from the National Endowment for the Humanities in 1994 and 1995. Currently she lives in California, where she writes, paints, plays music, and helps with her grandchildren.
www.susanegunter.com

www.ingramcontent.com/pod-product-compliance
Lightning Source LLC
LaVergne TN
LVHW041524070426
835507LV00012B/1794